A DICTIONARY OF
R.A.F. SLANG

We have many reasons for gratitude to the men of the Royal Air Force, and one of them is the colourful enrichment of the English language. By a fortunate chance – or an inspired calculation – they have had in their ranks since the beginning of the war Eric Partridge, widely recognized as one of the foremost authorities on the motives and history of slang. Mr. Partridge, author of the standard *Dictionary of Slang*, has made the most of his opportunity, and from his army experience of the last war, has been particularly well placed for purposes of comparison.

A Dictionary of R.A.F. Slang is as complete as any dictionary of a constantly expanding vocabulary can be, and, will take its place among indispensible books of its kind.

ERIC PARTRIDGE

A DICTIONARY OF
R.A.F.
SLANG

*With an
Introductory essay*

MICHAEL JOSEPH LTD.
an imprint of Penguin Books

MICHAEL JOSEPH

UK | USA | Canada | Ireland | Australia
India | New Zealand | South Africa

Michael Joseph is part of the Penguin Random House group of companies
whose addresses can be found at global.penguinrandomhouse.com.

First published 1945
This facsimile edition published 2016
002

Copyright © Eric Partridge, 1945

The moral right of the author has been asserted

Printed in Great Britain by Clays Ltd, St Ives plc

A CIP catalogue record for this book is available from the British Library

ISBN: 978–1–405–93059–8

www.greenpenguin.co.uk

Introduction

WORD-HISTORIES OF SOME R.A.F. SLANG[1]

1.[2] A long period of war—indeed, anything over six months—will always produce a crop of slang words, phrases, and sayings. Extremely little slang survives from the Napoleonic Wars, the Crimean War, the Indian Mutiny, and comparatively little from the Boer War; in those remote, those distant, those yester years, people omitted to think of collecting these attractive oddments. From the war of 1914–18, now unfortunately known as only the First World War, there survives, however, a mass of slang, both civilian and military. The same is happening this time.

2. In both the First and the Second World Wars it is noticeable that the Combatant Services have a far richer *new* slang than that used by the civilians. Nor is the reason difficult to ascertain. In the Services, the men live—or should live—a more exciting life; they deal with new equipment and various weapons; do things they've never done before—and pretend they never want to again; many of them visit strange countries; many become engaged in a service that is actually instead of nominally active; all of them mingle in such a companionship as they have never had before they enlisted and will never again have, once they quit the Service.

3. Such conditions inevitably lead to a rejuvenation of language—to vividness—to picturesqueness—to vigour; language becomes youthful, energetic, adventurous. And slang is the easiest way to achieve those ends; that it is, very often, also the laziest way is irrelevant—nor, if it were relevant, would it much matter, for men

---

[1] Reprinted, by kind permission, from *The Nineteenth Century and After*, April 1944.

[2] The numbers are for easy reference from Dictionary to Introduction.

speaking vigorously and vividly will not stop at slang: Standard English itself becomes refreshed and enriched.

4. But how do the slangs of the three Services compare one with another? The richest of all is that of the Army; yet the Army has added only a small number of words and phrases to those inherited from the First World War. The Navy's slang, not quite so extensive as that of the Army, is even more traditional. The Air Force had a small body of slang even when it was the Royal Flying Corps. The R.A.F. has many more slang terms than were possessed by the R.F.C., although the total number of its terms is very much smaller than those of the two senior Services. The R.A.F. still employs a few words that were in use so long ago as 1914–18; these few, however, are used either only or mainly by the men over forty or in new senses, one of the latter being *erk*, to which we shall shortly return.

5. Although R.A.F. slang is so much smaller numerically than Army slang and Navy slang, it is no less virile and picturesque and amusing; in the mass, it is, in fact, more amusing. Not that I find *he's had it*, or any of its variations, particularly amusing: this catch phrase is used far too much, often with very little point—if with any. The origin of this phrase is extremely obscure, and probably we shall never discover it. I think that it is short for *he has had his issue*—that which he is entitled to be issued with from the stores; or there may be a reminiscence of the old *I've had some* (I know by experience) or even of *I'm not having any* (I am having —and shall have—nothing to do with the matter).

6. It is not out of place to begin with ranks and trades. The Central Trade Test Board, by the way, is *the Brains Trust*, with reference to the Brains Trust of the B.B.C., which itself took the name from President Roosevelt's Brain Trust; the C.T.T.B., however, asks questions, not answers them. A Wing Commander becomes, by abbreviation, *Wingco*; rather similar is *Groupy* for Group Captain; and, though in its termination only, *Chiefy*, Flight Sergeant (collo-quially *Flight*), resembles *Groupy*; although its history is much more

interesting, *Chiefy* dating from the days when the Naval Air Service rank of the man discharging duties similar to those of a Flight Sergeant held the rank of *Chief* Petty Officer. *Stationmaster*—obviously from the terminology of railways—is an officer commanding an *operational* R.A.F. station. The Meteorological Officer is *Met* or *Mets*, the Education Officer is *Schooly*—borrowed from the Army and representing the old title of *Army Schoolmaster*. Talking of borrowings, we may, while we're on the subject, mention *mouldy*, a torpedo, which has been 'common form' in the Navy since the beginning of the century; in dialect, *mouldy* is a mole—hence the origin of the Fleet Arm's use of the term; and the R.A.F.'s motto, 'Muck you, Jack; I'm fire-proof,' which merely adapts the century-old Naval motto, 'Muck you, Jack; I'm all right.'

7. But to return to ranks and trades. *Corp* and *Sarge* are old Army terms of address. *Plumber* is an armourer. *Op*, an operator; hence *Wop*, a wireless operator, from the abbreviation, *W.Op.*, and therefore not to be confused with the American-slang *Wop*, an Italian. In 1914–18 and for some years afterwards, an *erk*, now used for an A.C.2 or for a 'Sprog,' meant an air mechanic. This odd word is, the writer believes, a shortened pronunciation of the italicized letters in '*air* me*chanic*' (probably in the form 'air mech') and the philological degradation—or perhaps merely the mutation—would be:

> *air mechanic*
> *air mech* (pronounced *mek*)
> *airmch*
> *airch*
> *erk;*

some airmen less convincingly hold that it comes from 'lower de*ck* hand,' yet others that the origin lies in the *irk*some jobs they often have to do. Much the same kind of thing, with the addition of one of those ingenious twists beloved by the slangy, has happened in *sprog*, the R.A.F.'s word for the Army's *rooky* or recruit. *Sprog* comes from '*frog sp*awn,' spawn that, like the recruit, is very, very green, thus: the two sets of italicized letters are transposed; *rogsp* would be intolerably difficult to pronounce; but by reversal we

8

obtain sprog.[1] *Sprog* is also used as an adjective, to mean new or inexperienced or, as in 'a sprog corporal,' recently appointed.

8. Of the slang names for particular bodies of men, we may select those for the Service Police: on some stations they are known as *Snoops* or *Snoopers*, which, from to *snoop* or spy, is unkind; on others as the *Gestapo*, which is merely satirical of a much-hated German special police-force. More amusing is *the Chain Gang*, men of all work—those helots of the R.A.F.: the A.C.H.s-G.D. (Aircrafthands, general duties): in allusion to the one-time chaining together of convicts engaged on roadwork.

9. Thence to weapons, equipment, apparatus. A *chatterbox* is a machine-gun, from its rattling talk with *confetti* (as a stream of *ammo* or ammunition is called); a *hip-flask* is a revolver, from the position in which it is often carried; a *Mae West* is a safety-jacket —worn, it bulges in the right places. The *intercom* is the inter-communication telephone system of a plane.

10. A plane is now a kite, whereas in 1914–18 it used to be a *bus* or, as often it still is, a *crate*; the first and the third of these terms constitute excellent examples of British meiosis or understatement. Many types of plane have either a nickname or a slang name. Most of these names are obvious; for instance, *Spit* and *Hurry* and *Cat* (a Catalina); slightly less obvious, though presenting no difficulties. are *Lizzie* for a Lysander and *Maggie* for a Miles *Ma*gister; more picturesque is *Limping Annie* (often *Annie*, for short), the Anson, from the unevenness of its engine-note. Among German places, we have *He, Me and You*, a Heinkel, a Messerschmitt (also a *Messer*) and—German *ju* being pronounced *you*—a Junkers. A Dornier is a *Doe*, a Henschel a *Hen*, both by puns on the official abbreviations, *Do.* and *Hen.* The Focke-Wulf fighter planes have been very aptly named *The Abbeville Kids* from the two facts, that our airmen first

---

[1] It must, however, be mentioned that R.A.F. folklore attributes *sprog* to a recruit's wholly unintentional blending (said to have occurred in 1930) of '*sprocket*' and '*cog*' and to the wildfire popularity of the error. 'Se no è vero è ben trovato.'

met them over or near Abbeville and that, like the Dead-End Kids of cinematic fame, they have no very rosy future.

11. From planes we naturally pass to operations (slangily *ops*) and activities. *Circuits and bumps* are those frequently repeated take-offs, circlings and landings which are practised at the E.F.T.S. or Elementary Flying Training School; the landings tend to be excessively bumpy. To *footle around* is to circle in search of a target, this—to adventurous spirits—being a waste of time; the word *footle* is from *futile* in its alternative pronunciation *futil*. To *go through the gate* is to open the throttle full out. To *be tangled in the soup* is to be lost or at the least in difficulties in a fog, suggested by the Londoner's *pea-souper* for a thick, yellowish fog. To 'bale out' (strictly speaking to make a parachute-landing) is to *jump out of the window*, either on to *the deck* or land or into *the drink* or sea. *The deck*, originally used by Naval airmen, was prompted by *the drink* (adopted from sailors' slang); *the Big Drink* is a fifty-years-old nautical term for the Atlantic. If one cannot *keep one's tail clear*—that is, out of the enemy's gun-sights—one may qualify for the epitaph, *He's gone for a Burton*, literally, for a glass of ale, which is the R.A.F.'s form of *he's gone West*. Derivatively, *he's gone for a Burton* means that he is absent (compare the Army's *Up in Annie's room*); a yet later derivative use is of things: for instance, a button that is missing may be said to have gone for a Burton. To depart, especially if hurriedly to oppose raiding enemy planes, is to *scat*, which is short for 'to scatter,' much as the American *scram* is short for 'scramble.' A *scramble* is a fight in the air, which may also be described as a *party*, a good time being had by all; the former term is more properly applied to what we used to call a 'dog fight,' an aerial 'free-for-all.' Comparable with *party* is to *go to the movies*, to go into action: one sees some remarkable pictures. In action, one may bomb the *Crump Dump* or Ruhr, in which our airmen have made so many 'crump holes' or bomb-craters; in 1914–18, a *crump* was the shell (or its explosion) of a German 5.9. To bomb a place, especially to bomb it heavily, is to *prang* it; *prang* may be a blend of to 'paste' and *bang*. Hence, if an airman bumps into a door or a wall or a chair or what-have-you, he says he has *pranged* it. A fairly regular

early-morning bombing of a specific target is a *milk-round*; compare a *piece of cake*, an easy raid, an easy victory in an air battle: as easy to 'take' as a cake, and as pleasant. Compare also *cookie*, a 4,000 or 8,000 lb. bomb, ironically agreeable for the recipients to digest.

12. Information concerning operations (or anything else) is *gen*; not, as many suppose, from 'genuine,' for, if that were the correct origin, why should we speak of *pukka gen*, authentic or correct information? Of *phoney gen*, doubtful information? And of *duff gen*, incorrect information? *Pukka*, as in *pukka sahib*, is from Hindustani; *duff*, probably connected with *dough*, has been adopted from the English underworld, '*duff* goods' being trashy or, at the least, inferior; *phoney* from the American underworld, which adapted it from *fawney*, the English underworld term for a ring, the transition being effected by 'Brum' jewellery. No; *gen* is from 'for the *gen*eral information of all ranks,' common to the three Services.

13. Those three phrases for three different kinds of information spring from an attitude of mind or perhaps only from a mood. Which brings us to several other terms expressive of mood or attitude. *To shoot down in flames* or *to shoot down from a great height* (both obviously from aerial warfare) is to defeat a person in an argument, a discussion, whereas *to shoot a line* is to boast or to talk too much, this phrase coming perhaps from the dropping of a stick of bombs in a straight and accurate line. To *bind* a person is to bore him stiff; probably from the ill-temper that so often results from being *bound* or constipated. Hence, by a not unnatural transition, we say that 'So-and-so was binding all the morning'; that is, grumbling or complaining or finding fault or merely being a nuisance, a bore. A person or a thing that is a bore or a nuisance is a *bind*, but one who is a grouser or a fault-finder is termed a *binder*. *Binding* (or grousing) may spring from being *browned off*, *cheesed off*, *brassed off*, or what used to be called 'fed up.' *Browned off* originated, somewhere about 1932, in the Regular Army in India; it comes from cooking, a dish that is over-baked being browned off the menu; there may also be a reminiscence of 'to be in a brown

11

study,' depressed or low-spirited. *Cheesed off* was probably suggested by *browned off*; the link is to be found in the *brown* or brownish rind of *cheese*. *Brassed off* is originally a Naval term, which derives from the excessive, or very frequent, polishing of the ship's brass-work. *Brassed off* is not much used by the R.A.F., which is beginning to make *cheesed off* its favourite among these three phrases.

But lest *you* should become 'cheesed off' . . .

A

Abbeville Kids, the   Focke-Wulf 'planes and/or the pilots thereof. (See *Introduction*, para. 10.)

ac   Accumulator. Mostly electricians'.

A.C. Plonk   An Aircraftman, 2nd Class. *Plonk* is echoically allusive to mud: and 'his name is mud.' Cf. **erk**.

ack-ack   Anti-aircraft gun(s) or fire. (Common to all three Services. Signalese.)

Adje, the   The Adjutant. (Adopted from the Army; from the abbreviation *Adj*.)

Admiral, the   That officer who has charge of the boats in the Air-Sea Rescue Service.

Air Commode   Air Commodore.

Air House, the   The Air Ministry. On military *War House*, the War Office.

airmaids   The crew of an Air-Sea Rescue boat.

ammo   Ammunition. (Adopted from the Army.)

anchor   One who waits too long to drop by parachute.

Annie   See **Limping Annie**. The form *old Annie* is falling into disuse.

apron   A hangar's tarmac surround. Partly from the colour, partly from the fact of surrounding.

Are you happy in—or at—your work?   A catch-phrase addressed ironically or facetiously to a Serviceman (or woman) performing some heavy or disagreeable or notoriously unsuitable task.

arrival   A clumsy or otherwise defective landing. The pilot has landed—but that's all.

13

Arse-end Charlie Richard Hillary, *The Last Enemy*, 1942, 'Arse-end Charlie is the man who weaves backwards and forwards above and behind the [usually the Fighter] Squadron, to protect them from attack from the rear.' Contrast *tail-end Charlie*.

artic See Queen Mary.

attaboy A member of the Air Transport Auxiliary, many of whom are Americans; and *attaboy!*, 'go it!', is American.

aviate To show off while one is flying a 'plane.

B

bag A parachute. From its shape while it is unopened.

bag, v. To shoot down, whether from the air or by A.A. fire. From sportsmen's slang.

bags of Very much of; a great amount of. Especially in *bags of bull*, excessive spit-and-polish and/or parades, inspections, and exasperating details and petty duties, and *bags of panic*, a pronounced state of nervousness or 'dithers.' Adopted from civilian slang.

Balbo 'A large formation of aircraft, so called after the famous flight of the Italian air armada from Italy to South America, led by the late Marshal of that name' (Hunt and Pringle, *Service Slang*, 1943).

bale out To make a parachute landing. (Colloquial.)

balloonatic A member of Balloon Command. A blend of *balloon* and *lunatic*.

banana boat An aircraft-carrier, according to the R.A.F. To soldiers it means an invasion barge.

bandstand A cruet in the Officers' Mess. From the shape: adopted from the Army.

bang on! All right! Correct! In Bomber Command: from a bomb dropped *bang on* (exactly on) the target.

basher This word is, in combination, fast becoming: man, chap, fellow. Cf. **stores basher.**

beam See **on the beam.**

beat up, v.; **beat-up,** n. A ground-strafing; to ground-strafe.

  (2) To stunt-fly, at low level, about (a place); such a stunt-flight.

  (3) Hence, a brisk evening in mess, or at a public-house.

Beau A Beaufighter.

beef To bore one's fellows by giving Queen-Anne information or talking very dry 'shop.' Cf. **bind.**

beehive A very close formation of bombers (the hive) with an escort of fighters (the bees flying about the hive).

Beer-Barrel A Buffalo 'plane.

beer-lever The 'joystick' of an aircraft. From pub-bars.

beetle-juice Betelgeux—'one of the stars which with Sirius and Procyon form a huge equilateral triangle. The star is bright red and easily distinguishable. It is aircrew slang' (C. H. Ward-Jackson, *It's a Piece of Cake*, The Sylvan Press, 1943—an excellent book of—and on—R.A.F. slang).

Belinda A frequent nickname of barrage balloons.

belly Undercarriage of an aircraft. See **quick squirt** and:—

belly-landing or **belly-flop** A landing effected with the wheels unlowered.

billed Briefed; detailed in Orders. From the theatre.

bind, n. A thing, person, duty, etc., that is either tedious or a nuisance.

bind, v. To bore or be a nuisance to. 'Drill binds me rigid.' *Introduction*, para. 13.

  (2) Intransitively: to be given to excessive complaints; to be officious in the discharge of one's duty—especially a nuisance to one's subordinates.

  (3) To be, with sickening frequency, 'in the swim—in the know.'

binder One who complains unduly.

binders Brakes of an aircraft.

binding Boring; tedious.

       (2) Given to excessive complaint.

Bishop, the The Padre.

black A blunder; a task or duty done badly. From the '*black* mark' one got for it.

black box or gen box Instrument that enables bomb-aimer to see through clouds or in the dark.

black-outs A pair of W.A.A.F. knickers or pantees; properly, the navy-blue winter-weights. How fascinating, yet how dependable, are semantics! An illuminating parallel to *black-out* in this derivative sense is the old story of the girl that her lover surprised 'making a pair of window-blinds for her sitting-room.' Contrast and compare **twilights.**

black, put up a The officers' version of the airmen's 'to *boob.*' See **black.**

black show A 'poor show.' Cf. **black.**

Blenburgher A Blenheim bomber. Punning *hamburgher*—the word and the shape.

blister An excrescence that, on a 'plane, serves to enclose and house a machine-gun or a cannon.

blitz That cleaning of barracks and buttons which takes place when a 'big noise' is expected to arrive at a station. As a verb, it = to reprimand a subordinate; cf. the *strafe* of 1914-18. (Both Army and R.A.F.)

blitz buggy An ambulance—so useful in a 'blitz.'

       (2) A very fast vehicle. From the literal sense of the German word, 'lightning.'

blitz, solid lump of A large, close-flying formation of enemy aircraft.

blonde job A fair-haired 'Waaf.'

blood chit Any written authorization that 'covers' or protects the bearer; earlier (and still), a ransom note carried by the members of air-crews flying over hostile or doubtful

16

territory in the East. Also known as a *gooly chit*: *goolies* are testicles: a common form of native torture consists in the excision of a man's testicles.

blood-wag(g)on   An ambulance. Less general: *blood tub*.

blower   An aircraft supercharger. From the Naval sense, 'telephone' or, rather, the speaking-tube connecting Bridge and Engine-Room.

bluebird   A 'Waaf.' From the blue bird of happiness: she could give it.

bobbing   Favour-currying with a superior. (*To bob* is, of course, to drop a curtsey.)

bod   Short for *body* in its official sense, 'a person actually available —not merely present on the paper strength of a unit, detachment, etc.'

body-snatcher   A stretcher-bearer.

bogey   An aircraft suspected to be hostile.

bomber boy   Any member of the aircrew of a bomber 'plane. (Colloquial.)

bomb up, v.i. and v.t.   To load (an aircraft) with bombs: colloquial. Hence vbl.n., *bombing-up*.

boob   To make a blunder: 'Someone has boobed.' From the n. *boob*, 'a fool,' itself from *booby*.

borrow   To take; to appropriate; to purloin. Cf. the Army's *win* and Shakespeare's *convey*.

bought it, or **bought a packet, he**   He was shot down, especially if through carelessness or recklessness.

bound rigid   See **bind**, v.

bowser king, the   The N.C.O. in charge of the bowser or petrol tanker used for the refuelling of aircraft.

box clever   To use one's head in order to avoid an undesirable task or duty, or to 'wangle' out of an unwelcome posting or attachment.

Brains Trust, The   The Central Trades Test Board, which examines candidates for a higher classification. *Introduction*, para. 6.

brassed off or **browned off** or **cheesed off**   Much depressed, in low spirits; disgruntled. (See *Introduction*, para 13.) To most airmen, all three are equally strong; to a few, the first is the weakest, the second the strongest expression.

break van   A mobile van from which, at morning or afternoon 'break,' tea and cakes are served.

Bricks or **Bricks and Mortar**   The Works Department of the Air Ministry—often known by its initials: A.M.W.D.

bride   A fellow's girl friend (not necessarily a sexual intimate).

Brock's benefit   A very bright display of flares, searchlights, and A.A. fire.

brolly   A parachute. (From the appearance of the 'chute if it has fully opened. Hence, *brolly hop*, a parachute-jump. Cf. **jump out of the window.**)

brown   An error; a 'poor show.' Also *brown show*. Less discreditable than a *black*.

Brown Job, the   The Army. A *brown job* is a soldier; a *brown type* is also a soldier—but usually an officer.

brown Windsor Soap   From *Windsor* soap, which is brown—and a frequent issue to airmen.

bubble-dancing   Washing one's 'irons' and, at some stations, plates.

bucket   A bucket-shaped formation of aircraft in the air.

bull   See **bullshit.**

bullshit   Often shortened to *bull* or *bulsh*. Excessive 'spit and polish' or attention to detail; regimentalism. Hence, *Bullshit morning*, that morning on which the C.O.'s inspection takes place.

(2) Originally, a spate of official talk—as advice, deterrent, or eyewash. Still a common sense; it comes from the U.S.A.

bumf (not **bumph**) Leaflets dropped from the air. From the Army's sense, current as early as 1914–18, 'official correspondence; Army forms,' itself from *bumfodder* (toilet paper).

bumfleteers or **bumphleteers** Airmen engaged in dropping pamphlets on enemy or enemy-occupied territory. A blend of *bumf* and *pamphleteers*.

bumps See **circuits and bumps.**

bunk A small Corporals' Barrack Room, usually just outside Men's Barrack Room. It contains three bunks of beds; the corporals *bunk down* (or 'kip' or sleep) there.

Burton See **gone for a Burton.**

bus, an aircraft, is a survival, now little used, from airmen's slang of 1914–18.

bus-driver A bomber pilot. He often travels the same route.

buttoned-up See **wrapped up.**

buttoned-up In good order; well prepared. (From the Army.)

buzz A rumour.

C

cabbage A bomb. *Sow* (one's) *cabbages* is to drop one's bombload. Cf. **groceries.**

cake-hole Mouth.

camp is a colloquialism—now almost jargon—for a station with or without airfield—a unit's or detachment's location—a training school—a depot—or even a landing-ground. Not, however, applied to any such place if it is situated in a town.

Camp Comedian A Camp Commandant.

canteen cowboy A ladies' man. From the American synonym, *drug-store cowboy*.

carry the can To take due blame or to accept blame for another's mistake or crime. Common to all three Services, the phrase relates to that member of a gang or a party who fetches the beer for all.

Cas, the The Chief of Air Staff. From the abbreviation *C.A.S.*

Cat Catalina ('plane).

cat's eyes A particularly keen-eyed pilot. Adopted from the newspapers and, in the R.A.F., generally used jocularly or derisively.

cat's walk A long plank that, on a bomber, runs from cabin to tail. A development of the 1914–18 Army's sense, a duckboard pathway.

Chain Gang, the Aircrafthands, General Duties: The R.A.F.'s maids of all work. (See *Introduction*, para. 8.)

chair-borne division, the R.A.F. personnel working in offices. Ironic on *air-borne division*.

champagne glass A Hampden—also, though less frequently— a Hereford 'plane in the plan-view.

char Tea. From Hindustani (itself from Chinese) *tchai*, whence *tea* itself. Adopted from the Army. This large-scale borrowing from the Army's rich slang may be further illustrated by the fact that, at the daily break (theoretically 10.30–11 a.m.), you may, in the R.A.F., hear many an airman ask for 'char and a wad,' *wad* being a cake or a bun or a scone. *Wad* may allude to that wad which was used in the old muzzle-loading guns.

chatterbox A machine-gun. (See *Introduction*, para. 9.)

check To reprimand, take to task, during the exercise of one's duty. Proleptic: reprimanding should have the effect of causing the reprimandee to check his evil or mistaken ways cr to correct his mistake.

Chiefy Flight Sergeant. (See *Introduction*, para. 6.)

chin-food A *binder's* talk.

chippy A carpenter. Common to all three Services, it has been adopted from civilian slang. From the chips and shavings of wood. Whence *chippy-rigger*, a carpenter rigger.

chocks away! Let's make a start! Once the chocks have been removed, the 'plane can rise from the ground.

chute A parachute. (Colloquial.)

circuit-and-bump boys Pupil pilots. From:—

circuits and bumps Those circuits and landings which are so assiduously practised by aspirant pilots. (See *Introduction*, para. 11.) By itself, *bumps* = any faulty or bumpy landing caused by, e.g., unfavourable weather.

civvies Civilian clothes. (Adopted from the Army.)

civvy A recruit, so long as he is still in civilian clothes.

Civvy Street Civilian life, but especially one's own pre-enlistment civilian life. Adopted from the Army. Here, *street* = sphere of activity or occupation or condition, as in *He's in Queer Street* (on the verge of bankruptcy).

civvy kip One's civilian bed. (Adopted from the Army.)

clock basher or **watch basher** An instrument maker or repairer—as a 'trade' in the R.A.F. See **basher.**

Close hangar doors!; hangar doors closed! Stop talking shop!

club A propeller.

clueless Without knowledge (about something specific), as in 'Invasion? I'm clueless!'; ignorant, especially in *clueless type*—the opposite of a *gen man*.

collect a gong To be awarded a decoration. *Gong* is Army slang for a medal.

comb out To make an extensive, ground-target sweep with gunfire over (a territory). (Colloquial.)

come to town; generally in 'They're coming to town.' Applied to enemy aircraft approaching.

come up! 'Put some service in!' On time-promotion lists, the short-service men are naturally at the bottom.

coming and going Applied to a 'plane that is fitted with a wireless set.

con course A conversion course, taken by a person desirous of changing from one 'trade' to another.

(2) Hence, the substitution of one type of armament for another on a 'plane.

confetti Machine-gun fire. (Adopted from America; not very general.)

conk Synonymous with—and actually a shortening of—the 1914–18 airmen's *conk out*, to cease from functioning, hence also to die.

conservatory Cabin of a 'plane. From the perspex on three sides of the pilot.

cookie A 4,000-lb. bomb; hence, also an 8,000-pounder. (See *Introduction*, para. 11, at end.)

cooler A guard or detention room. Adopted from the Army. It cools beery ardour.

cope To be able to deal with a duty, task, difficulty. 'It's a tricky job, but I'm coping.'

court a cat Take a girl friend out.

crab An A.V. Roe trainer 'plane. (The 504.)

crab; crab along To fly near the ground; synonymous with the now Standard English *hedge-hop*.

crack (a 'plane) **down** To shoot (it) down.

crack down on (the deck) or **in (the drink)** To crash-land on the ground or into the sea.

(2) Hence, to make a forced landing.

crack-up An accident causing only repairable damage. Perhaps from *crack up*, to become exhausted.

crafty Skilful; clever, cunning, well-judged, well-timed; well-planned.

crate A 'plane. (See *Introduction*, para. 10.) Its 1939–45 meaning is: an obsolescent, almost obsolete 'plane.

crib To complain; *crib at*, complain about. Hence, *crib*, that of or about which one complains. Adopted from stable slang and almost equally common in the Army.

cricket A German night-fighter 'plane.

crook and butcher Facetious for cook and butcher.

crown, to have got one's To have been promoted to Flight Sergeant. A F/S wears a crown above his three stripes. (Colloquial.)

Crump Dump, the The Ruhr. (See *Introduction*, para. 11.)

crump hole Bomb crater. (See *Introduction*, para. 11.)

crumper A heavy crash. 'The Messer came a crumper.' Echoic.

cu Cumulus cloud. From the official abbreviation.

D

Daffy A Defiant ('plane). By the process of 'Hobson-Jobson.'

daisy cutter A faultless landing. From cricket, where it = a drive clean along the sward.

dawn hopper An enemy 'plane availing itself of the morning half-light to set off for home.

dead stick Applied to an engine that has given out.

deck, the The land. (*Introduction*, para. 11.) From the old R.N.A.S.

dedigitate See **pull your finger out.**

depth charge A prune. In the Services, prunes are provided as a mild and not unpleasant laxative.

dim type A stupid—or, at the least, a dense—fellow. Originally. *dim* was Oxford University slang.

dim view See **take a dim view.**

dirt Anti-aircraft fire.

ditch, the The sea; especially the English Channel. (Adopted from nautical slang.)

ditch, to Cf. **drink.** To make a forced landing. E.g., into a ditch.

do you want—occasionally an abrupt **want**—**to buy a battleship?** A catch-phrase equivalent to 'Do you want to make water,' often addressed to a man that one has playfully awakened. An interrogatory elaboration of *pump ship*, 'to urinate.'

Doe A Dornier 'plane. (See *Introduction*, para. 10.)

dog A sausage. Common to all three Services. From the common superstition that all stray dogs become sausage meat.

dog clutch A disconnectable coupling. (Aircrews'.)

draw a pint To use the 'joystick.' Cf. **beer-lever,** for the semantics.

drill The correct way of doing anything. 'That's the drill.'—'He knows his drill.' Adopted from the Army.

drink, the The sea. (See *Introduction*, para. 11.)

drive the train The phrasal verb that corresponds to **train-driver.**

Driver A pilot. Taken over from the R.N.A.S.

drome An aerodrome. (Colloquial.) (*Aerodromes* are now *airfields*, precisely as—officially—an *aeroplane* is now an *aircraft*.)

dromestoners Lit., those who remove stones from an incipient airfield. With a reminiscence of *barnstormers*.

drone An air gunner, whether in dorsal turret or—cf. **tail-end Charlie**—in rear turret. For hours he does nothing—and then—oh, boy!

dual Colloquial for dual-control flying instructions.

dud weather Weather unfit for aerial-bombing operations.

duff To render unserviceable, unusable, unwearable; to ruin; to destroy. From the originally underworld *duff*: very inferior; worthless.

duff gen False or grossly inaccurate information. See **gen.**

duffy To polish (e.g. one's buttons). Origin?

dustbin A rear-gunner's turret: the rear-gun gets the 'dirt' from attacking enemy 'planes, and the turret is shaped much like a dustbin.

(2) Hence, 'a gun-position on the under-side of the fuselage' (Hunt and Pringle).

E

egg A bomb; but also—see the next entry—a mine. In the former sense, it dates from the days of the R.F.C.

eggs, lay To lay mines (in enemy waters). In the War of 1914–18, it meant 'to drop bombs.'

egg-whisk An autogyro. From its motions.

Elsan gen Untrustworthy news; synonymous, therefore, with *phoney gen*. See **gen** and, especially, para. 12 of the *Introduction*; *Elsan* is the trade name of the chemical w.c. with which bombers are fitted.

embark leave Embarkation leave.

Engines Engineering Officer; hence, Technical Officer. (Mostly officers'.)

'Erb A term of address to any airman. But then, so is *George* or *Jack*.

erk (For the origin, see *Introduction*, para. 7.) A recruit; an A.C.2, at no matter what stage of his 'apprenticeship.' Hence, loosely: an A.C.1.

Everything (or **Everything's**) **under control** All is going well. Adopted from Big Business.

Eyetie An Italian 'plane. From the Army's *Eyetie*, an Italian.

F

fan Propeller. From its functional activity: it then somewhat resembles an electric fan.

fiddle (Generally used intransitively.) To 'wangle.'

fiddler An expert at 'wangling'—a 'smart guy.'

fire-proof Invulnerable. See **muck you**.

fireworks Heavy A.A. fire. (2) Hence, intensive flare-dropping.

fit   Only in *Are you fit?*, are you ready? Perhaps elliptical for 'Are you ready and fit?'

fizzer, the   Mostly in *put*, or *be put*, *on the fizzer*, to put a man, or to be put, on a charge. Perhaps to (cause to) 'fizz' with anger or resentment.

(2) The guard room; a detention room; a confinement-to-camp.

flaming onions   Anti-aircraft tracer shells and/or bullets.

flanker   See **play a flanker**.

flannel; to flannel; flanneller   (To use) flattering or wheedling words, (to make) gifts to one's superiors in order to ask favours; one who does this. Flannel is soft (cf. *soft soap*) and soothing.

flannelling, n.   The practice or exercise of such flattery: see preceding entry.

flap   Panic; excitement; disturbance. 'There's a flap on' means that an air-raid is either expected or in progress. Adopted from the Army, which got it from the Navy. From a bird's wing-flapping prior to alarmed flight. Hence:—

flap, to   To be excessively nervous; to panic. (See the preceding entry.)

flat out for, be   To think very highly of; to favour. 'I'm flat out for his promotion.' Perhaps from *flat out*, 'at full speed' (itself from motor racing).

flat spin, to be in or **go into a**   To be so busy, have so many things to do, that one doesn't 'know where one is.' From a 'plane that is out of control. A survival from the Air Force slang of 1914–18.

Fleet Air Arm wallah   See **matlo**.

flicks   Searchlights. For the semantics, cf. **movies**.

Flight   Flight Sergeant. (Colloquial.)

Flight Louie   A Flight Lieutenant. From 'loo'tenant.'

Flight magician A flight mechanic. From the wonderful things—some of them unorthodox—he does with his hands.

fling (or **sling**) or **throw one up** To give a salute. From the movement.

flip A short flight in a 'plane; especially one that is accorded to a friend.

flit commode A Flight Commander. Cf. **air commode.**

float around To fly for fun or to pass the time, in a leisurely manner, near one's objective or journey-end.

flyblow A flying boat.

Flying Cigar A Wellington bomber 'plane, especially as seen from the side. Cf.:—

Flying Pencil A Dornier bomber (likewise in side-view).

Flying Suitcase or **Tadpole** A Hampden Bomber (properly as viewed laterally).

Flying Tin-Opener A Hurricane 'plane employed as a tank-buster.

fog See **Scotch mist.**

fold up, to (Of a 'plane) to crash suddenly or unexpectedly.

(2) Hence (of a person): to report sick. Probably from the action of a defective parachute.

football feet, to have To make excessive use of the rudder.

footle around To circle in search of a target. (See *Introduction*, para 11.)

for 'Brighton' read 'tight un' An old Service catch-phrase imputing drunkenness.

fore-and-aft A field, as distinct from a dress, service cap.

foreigner An article (e.g. a model 'plane) made of R.A.F. material. Adopted by Air Force and Army from civilian workers.

Fort Flying Fortress. (Colloquial.)

fix, v.i. To do something clever or cunning; especially to dog, cunningly, an enemy 'plane.

Freeman, Hardy, and Willis or, much more general, *Pip*, *Squeak*, *and Wilfred*. The 1914–15 Star, the Overseas Service, and the Victory Medals of the last war, or the three respective ribbons worn on the tunic's left breast. The former phrase: from the three inseparable names of an extremely well-known firm of boot-and-shoe merchants. The latter: from the three comic-strip characters of the children's page of a 'national' newspaper. If the first medal (the 1914–15) be missing, the other two are known as *Mutt and Jeff*—from two cinematic cartoon characters of about 1919–21. The second and third of these phrases have come to the R.A.F. from the Army.

frozen on the stick Paralysed with fear. (This is the 'joy-stick' or control-lever.)

fruit salad A large number of medal ribbons (worn over the left breast).

full bore 'Flat out'—at full speed.

G

gaspirator A Service anti-*gas* res*pirator*. Adopted from the Army.

gat A revolver; a machine-gun. From the American underworld: short for *Gatling gun*.

gate, go through the To open the throttle full out in order to fly at the 'plane's maximum speed. Synonymous with *turn up the wick*.

gen Information (see para. 12 of the *Introduction*).

(2) Hence: notes on procedure; notes for a course, a test, an examination. 'My gen book is O.K.'

(3) By way of *pukka gen*: an adjective meaning 'genuine' or (of a place, a station) 'very pleasant.' E.g., '*This* news is gen'; 'He likes X station: it's gen.'

gen book See gen (2) and cf.:—

gen file A general file—i.e., general to a particular department (or branch thereof) or containing general matter or information on a particular activity or subject. Such a file contains genuine general *gen*.

gen box See black box.

gen king; gen wallah One who can be tapped for trustworthy information, especially concerning movements, operations, promotions, postings; particularly the N.C.O. in charge of the Orderly Room, or of the Operations Room, or of Signals.

gen man A clerk in the Orderly Room, or in Signals, or in the Operations Room. Cf. preceding entry.

gen up To 'swot' for a test or an examination; to read up a subject. Cf:—

genned up Well supplied with information. From **gen**, sense 1.

George Generic name for an airman.

(2) The automatic pilot. 'The saying "Let George do it" may well have suggested this name' (Hunt and Pringle, *Service Slang*, 1943).

Gestapo, the The Service Police. (See *Introduction*, para. 8.)

get (one's) blood back To shoot down that enemy 'plane which has caused the death of one's friend.

get cracking Get busy; bestir yourself! (Adopted from the Army.)

get mobile See mobile.

get organized See **organzied**.

get some flying hours in To obtain some sleep. Ironic. Cf. **homework**.

29

Get some time in!, often shortened to **get some in!** Serve longer in the Air Force before you talk—or act—in that way!

get up them stairs! A catch-phrase spoken to a man (especially if he is married) going on leave.

get weaving See **weaving.**

give her the gun To accelerate. *The gun* (from America) is the accelerator.

go and see a taxidermist! See **taxidermist.**

go into a flat spin See **flat spin.**

go snogging. See **snogging.**

go through the gate See **gate.**

go to the movies See **movies.**

goggled goblin A night-fighter pilot. Cf. **cat's eyes.**

Golden Eagle sits on Friday; the golden eagle lays its egg(s). Next Friday is pay-day; it's pay parade.

gone for a Burton Dead. Derivatively: absent or (of things) missing. (See *Introduction*, para. 11.)

gone for six Killed; dead. From cricket.

goof A ladies' man. Because he's a fool to be one.

gong See **collect.**

gooly chit See **blood chit.**

goon A fool, very stupid fellow; a gaper. Perhaps a blend of *goof* and *loon.*

Gossage A barrage balloon. From A/M Sir Leslie Gossage, A.O.C. Balloon Command; with, also, a pun on *sausage.*

grab for altitude To try to get higher in the air, especially in a flight; hence, to become angry—very angry.

grand A thousand feet. 'Bandit at five grand' = an enemy aircraft at 5000 feet. From American-underworld *grand,* '1000 dollars.'

gravel-bashing Synonymous with **square-bashing.**

gravel-crusher. A P.T. Instructor; a Drill Instructor. Cf. preceding.

Gravy, the The Atlantic. (Pilots'.)

gravy Petrol. (A 'plane's nourishment.)

greenhouse A synonym of **conservatory.**

gremlin A mischievous sprite, by the R.A.F. held responsible for all mishaps. This excellent example of true folk-mythology is not slang, but genuine Standard English folklore. See C. H. Ward-Jackson, *It's a Piece of Cake*, 1943, for a masterly vignette on this Caliban-Ariel of the Junior Service.

G.R. navvy A general reconnaissance navigator.

grocer An Equipment Officer. Reputedly commercial.

groceries Bombs. Cf. its collective origin, **cabbage, cookie, egg,** etc.

grope A *gr*ound *op*erational *e*xercise.

grounded Often applied to a man newly married: he forgoes many of his bachelor activities; he can no longer be a '*fly*-by-night.'

ground-strafe; ground-strafing; ground-strafer To make a low-flying attack on gun-positions, trenches, transport; the practice or act of doing this; one who does—especially if he frequently does — this. (Colloquial.)

(2) Hence, to drive a M.T. vehicle in careless or reckless manner; the practice; the culprit.

ground wallah is a variant of **penguin.**

Grouper An officer on a Group H.Q. staff.

Groupy Group Captain.

Gussie An officer. (Familiar for *Augustus*, a 'tony' name.)

31

H

had it 'I've—you've—he's or she's—we've—you've—they've had it.' I'm too late, or unable to get it; the article, the promotion, the privilege is unobtainable. (For origin, see *Introduction*, para. 5.)

half-pint hero A boaster. One who exemplifies the virtue of Dutch courage without having the trouble of going into action.

Half-Ringer See **Ringer**.

half-section A mate or companion; hence, a friend or even one's wife.

Ham-Bone A *Ham*pden *Bomb*er.

hangar doors closed! See **close hangar doors!**

Happy Valley A much or frequently bombed area; especially the Ruhr. Ironic; or perhaps reminiscent of '*happy* hunting ground.'

He, me, and you (See *Introduction*, para. 10.)

heavy A heavy bomb or bomber. Ex Army, where it = a heavy gun or shell. (Colloquial.)

Hen Henschel 'plane. (See *Introduction*, para. 10.)

hip-flask A revolver. (See *Introduction*, para. 9.)

hit the deck To land. From the old R.N.A.S. days, when its meaning was literal.

hockey stick A bomb-loading jack or hoist. From a vague resemblance in shape.

hoick off To become airborne.

(2) Hence, to make—especially if promptly—one's way to some place.

hold everything! Leave off what you're doing—or, don't make any more plans—because something important has happened or some important news has come. Adopted from the U.S.A.

homework; a piece of homework (Of R.A.F. personnel) one's sweetheart or temporary girl friend. 'Oh, I have some homework—or, a piece of homework—to do (or, attend to).' Cf. **knitting.**

hoosh; hooshing To land—landing—at great speed. Echoic.

Hoover; Hoovering To make—the activity or practice of making—a fighter *sweep*. (From the Hoover cleaner.)

hop the twig To crash fatally. (Canadian pilots' and aircrews'.)

hot Fresh; very recent. Ex American '*hot* (up-to-the-minute) news.'

huffy A Waaf that is so superior as to refuse an airman's invitation.

hulk A (severely) damaged aircraft.

humdinger A fast 'plane (hence, vehicle); a smoothly running engine.

Hun A German 'plane. (Colloquial.)

Hurry A Hurricane 'plane.

Hurryback A Hurricane 'plane.

Hurry-buster A synonym of **Flying Tin-Opener.**

I

I.B.A. *I*gnorant *b*loody *a*ircrafthand. Perhaps reminiscent both of the *I.R.A.* and of the *P.B.I.* Cf. **Chain Gang** (q.v.).

I.C., the The officer, or the W.C.O., in charge; lacking officer or N.C.O., the senior man in, e.g., a barrack-room or a hut, or of a detachment, a squad. (Colloquial.) 'I must ask the I.C. about that; *he's* sure to know.'

in a spot In a difficult—especially if perilous—situation. An adaptation of the American underworld phrase *on the spot*.

in the blue On a lonely station; in a detachment far from other detachments; in the desert. Literally, in the blue air and therefore not on firm land.

incy See insy.

inoc Inoculation. 'He's just had his inoc for overseas, poor b—!'

insy properly *incy* (pronounced *insy*). Incendiary bomb.

intercom Intercommunication telephonic system of a 'plane.

irk Incorrect for *erk*.

iron lung Nissen hut. (Barrage Balloon personnel's.)

Irons Knife, fork, spoon. (Colloquial; short for *eating irons*.)

it's a piece of cake! See piece of cake. (The longer form provides the title of a very entertaining glossary of R.A.F. slang.)

J

Jabo Club, the That imaginary club to which belong all airmen *just about browned off*.

jam jar Armoured car. Rhyming slang. Adopted from the Army.

jankers Confinement to camp; fatigue and/or drill done as punishment. (Adopted from the Army, which took it over from the underworld. Originally, echoic in reference to chains: probably a corruption of *janglers*.)

Hence—both terms also borrowed from the Army—come:

(1) *jankers king, the*: the Provost Marshal or an Assistant Provost Marshal or a Deputy Assistant Provost Marshal; more generally, a Provost Sergeant or that N.C.O. who, whatever his rank, is in charge of the Service Police.

(2) *janker* (or *jankers*) *wallah*, any airman 'doing jankers' (undergoing punishment).

Jerry A German 'plane. From the 1914–18 sense, which survives: a German. Commoner than *Hun*, it was originally and more correctly *Gerry*.

Jim Crow The watch-out man while some unofficial activity is taking place during duty hours. From Civil Defence: in C.D., a roof-spotter.

jink, to; jinking; jinks To turn quickly and skilfully in the air in order to avoid enemy action; the activity or the practice of making these turns; the turns themselves. Also *jink away*, noun and verb.

job An aircraft. 'A very fast German job.'

(2) See **blonde job.**

Joe Soap An airman 'carrying the can' or doing work that should be done by another. Hence, *to Joe Soap*, to 'carry the can' for another or to do his work for him. *Joe Soap* rhymes *dope*, which, as in 'He's a regular dope,' is American slang for 'dolt' or 'softy' and probably represents a shortening of *dope-addict* rather than a variant of *dupe*.

join! A variant of **get some time in!**

joy Satisfaction. 'Any joy?' = Have you been successful? Have you obtained co-operation? Has (e.g.) he acceded to your request, met your demand, etc.?

joy-stick. See **stick.**

jug To drink. (The Army *jug*, 'detention or the guardroom,' is common in the R.A.F. also.)

Juice, the The North Sea. Cf. **drink** and contrast **gravy.**

jump on the binders To brake hard.

jump out of the window To make a parachute-landing.

K

keep one's tail clear To prevent an enemy 'plane from attacking one's *rear*.

kerdumf To crash into (cf. **prang**, v, 2). From *kerdumf!*, an interjection indicative of astonishment. Echoic: cf. the much older and mainly American *kerwallop!*

king The person in charge of whatever is denoted by the preceding word, as in **bowser king** and **jankers king**, qq.v., and as in *rations king*, the N.C.O. i/c rations, the messing clerk, or the Catering Officer.

35

kipper kites 'Planes protecting convoys in the North Sea (frequented by the *herring*-fishing fleets); by extension, in the Irish Sea. Original to and used mostly by Coastal Command.

kiss one's aircraft goodbye. To bale out.

kite. An aeroplane. (See *Introduction*, para. 10.)

kittens in a basket, or **like kittens** . . . (Extremely) friendly: applied by 'Waafs' to 'Waafs.'

kiwi A member of the ground staff: New Zealand airmen's, the kiwi being a non-flying New Zealand bird. Cf. **penguin.**

knitting; piece of knitting (Plural: *knitting* or *pieces of knitting*.) One's girl, or one's girls; girls collectively. Cf. the old civilian *skirt* (or *piece of skirt*) and the R.A.F. synonym, **homework.**

kweis or **kweiss** See **quis.**

L

ladybird A W.A.A.F. officer. To some airmen, all women are *birds*; to most airmen, the W.A.A.F. officers are *ladies*.

Lanky A Lancaster aircraft.

last three Colloquial (but fast becoming Standard English) for: last three figures of one's Service number. 'Full number, Flight?'—'No; your last three will do.'

lay eggs See **eggs, lay.**

lay on To arrange or appoint; to provide or render available. Adopted from the Army. Probably from plumbing.

leave visiting cards See **visiting card.**

left, right, centre To drop bombs right on the target, especially in its middle or centre and properly after a couple of experimental bomb-droppings.

(2) Hence, to do something correctly; e.g. to have one's belt-buckle dead in the middle of one's waist-line.

leg A hop—i.e., on long journeys, a stage between landings. From cribbage.

Limping Annie, often shortened to **Annie** An Anson 'plane. (See *Introduction*, para. 10.)

line-shoot A tall story or a piece of bragging. See **shoot a line.**

line-shooter A boaster or habitual exaggerator. From **shoot a line.**

lines book, or **shooting gallery** That book in which, at some 'camps,' are recorded the 'line-shoots' perpetrated by members of the Officers' Mess. The auditor makes the entry; a witness, if available, appends his corroborative signature.

Little Arthur Arsine (gas).

Lizzie A Lysander 'plane. Partly from the first three letters (*Lys*) and partly in reminiscence of motoring-slang *Lizzie* (or *tin Lizzie*), a Ford motor-car.

load bummer An obsolescent variant of **line-shooter.** The load is that in:—

load of guff An excess of sentiment, humbug, nonsense; 'hot air.'

loaf See **use your loaf!**

long-distance medal or **stripe; long-distance type** A medal or stripe for long service; an airman who has been in the Service for many years.

look-see A reconnaissance. Merely a specialization of the civilian colloquialism, adopted from pidgin, for 'a look' or what the soldier would call a 'dekko.'

loose off, v.i. or v.t. To fire from a machine-gun. 'He loosed off hundreds of rounds' or 'As soon as he caught sight of the Jerry on his tail, he just loosed off.'

37

M

maalish (pronounced **marleesh**)! It doesn't matter! 'san fairy Ann!' From the Arabic; adopted from the Army.

Macaroni An Italian; generally, an Italian aircraft. Borrowed from the Army.

made-up See **make-up**.

Mae West The safety-jacket worn by pilots and aircrews. (See *Introduction*, para. 9.) The term is now official.

Maggie A Miles *Mag*ister trainer 'plane. Cf. **Annie** and **Lizzie**.

make-up To promote (e.g., from Leading Aircraftman to Corporal). Not slangy, but colloquial.

marmalade That *gold*-coloured braid which adorns the hats of the mighty—Group Captains and those officers whose rank is even more astrological.

matlo; or **Fleet Air Arm wallah** A member of the Fleet Air Arm. For the second, see **wallah**. *Matlo* (or *matlow*), borrowed from the Navy, represents French *matelot*, 'a sailor.'

Me See He, Me and You in *Introduction*, para. 10.

meat waggon A variant of **blood waggon**. Cf. **blitz buggy**, which, by the way, is now used occasionally in official communications.

medico A Medical Officer. Not a blend but a direct adoption of the civilian colloquialism.

Mess or **Messer** A Messerschmitt 'plane. Cf. **Spit** and **Spitter**.

Met or **Mets** A Meteorological Officer. (The Army form of the word is *Met*.)

Mickey Mouse 'The bomb-dropping mechanism of some types of bomber aircraft is so called because it strongly resembles the intricate machinery portrayed in Walt Disney's cartoons' (Hunt and Pringle, *Service Slang*, 1943).

midwaaf or **midwaf** A Women's Auxiliary Air Force N.C.O. that is over-officious with her W.A.A.F. subordinates. Punning on *midwife* and implying interference.

milk round A run made fairly regularly by a Squadron or a Force, if it returns to its station or base in the early morning.

milk train The early-morning patrol (or 'recce' flight). Cf. the preceding entry.

mill or **mill around** Of a formation of aircraft: to fly in a self-protective circle; or, more generally, to fly, 'flat out,' in and out, so as to cross one another's path. Adopted from American airmen.

mobile especially in *get mobile*. Get moving; get busy; to attend promptly to a duty or to something in which one's profit or self-interest is involved. In contrast to *static*.

mod A modification, especially in the sense of a mechanical improvement. Colloquial. From the official abbreviation.

Mos (pronounced *moss*); **Mossy** Mosquito aircraft.

mouldy A torpedo. Adopted from the Navy, which has used the term since about 1900. (See *Introduction*, para. 6.)

mouse-trap See rat-trap.

movies, go to the Of airmen: to go into action. (See *Introduction*, para. 11.) Adopted from American airmen.

much! Not much!: ironic. ' "He never goes out with Waafs."—Much!" ': implying that he goes out very often with them.

muck (Very) dirty weather. Contrast **dirt**.

muck you, Jack, I'm fire-proof A frequently heard catch-phrase. (See *Introduction*, para. 6.)

mucking-in spud A friend with whom, in Army slang, one 'mucks in'—shares everything. *Spud:* perhaps from the Irish nickname, 'Spud (Murphy).'

muscle in To take advantage of another's good fortune or advantage. From the language of the American underworld, via the cinema.

muscle merchant A P.T. Instructor. The P.T.I.'s are usually strong and fit.

Mutt and Jeff See **Freeman, Hardy and Willis**.

N

Naffy or Narfy The N.A.A.F.I. (Common to all three Services.) Hence, *naffy-time*, a break—almost always in the morning—for refreshment at the Navy, Army and Air Force Institute; and *Naffy Romeo*, a ladies' man—addicted to treating W.A.A.F. personnel with Naffy refreshments.

Naffy gong 1939–43 star (medal). Since late 1943. For the semantics, cf. **rooty medal**. It is also called *the spam medal*.

natter To chatter. 'Stop nattering!' merely = 'Stop talking!' Perhaps a blend of *nag* and *chatter*. Hence the frequent verbal noun, *nattering*.

natter can A person—especially a 'Waaf'—prone to talk too much.

natter party A conference at which there is much talk of an inconclusive or useless kind.

navvy A navigator; often as a term of address.

Newton got him He crashed. See **Old Newton**.

N/I Not interested. Mostly officers'; with a pun on N/A, 'no action (necessary or taken); not available.'

niff-naff Generally 'Don't niff-naff!'—'Don't fuss, but get cracking!' Perhaps *naff* is reminiscent of *natter* and *fuss*, and *niff-naff* may be a reduplication of *naff*.

no (or there's no) **future at all**, sometimes with *in it* added. It's a dangerous job. An intensive of:—

no (or there's no) **future in it**. A catch-phrase that, among aircrews, is applied to a dangerous sortie, or attack. For the semantics, cf. **Abbeville Kids**.
  In this form, however, the phrase—cf. the preceding entry—sometimes means no more than that the work or undertaking is a thankless one.

nursemaid or nursemaids A fighter escort for bombers.

nursery An Elementary Flying-Training School.

nursery slope An easy target on which bombing-beginners practise. Cf. preceding entry.

O

observatory An astrodome—that part of an aircraft from which the navigator observes the stars.

octu An *O*fficer *C*adets' *T*raining *U*nit. (Colloquial.) See also **one-pause-two.**

office A 'plane's cabin or cockpit.

(2) Inside information. 'Do you know what the office is?' implies 'What is the information from Headquarters?' Cf. the civilian *give a person the office*, to inform him or give him a timely warning.

ogo-pogo, to Generally in the form of a verbal noun (*ogo-pogoing*) To seek an unidentified 'plane in order to identify it.

old Annie See **Annie** and **Limping Annie.** Also *old Faithful*, from its reliability.

old iron Spare copper coins that an airman doesn't object to hazarding in a gamble—a bet, a raffle, a card game.

Old Man, the The Commanding Officer. From the Army, which gets it from the Navy, which got it from the Merchant Service.

Old Newton The force of gravity, always tending to bring a 'plane to earth. From Isaac Newton, the discoverer of the laws of gravity.

on one's benders On one's knees; hence, very tired, exhausted, or —whatever the cause—unsteady on one's legs. *Benders* are knees because legs bend at the knees.

on one's jack (properly *Jack*). By oneself. Short for *on one's Jack Malone*, rhyming slang for 'on one's own.' A R.A.F. variant of the civilian on *one's Pat* (*Malone*).

on the beam I understand. To *be off the beam*, to fail to understand; to make a bad mistake.

on the fizzer See **fizzer.**

on the grim On the North-West Frontier of India. Since ca. 1920. It *is* 'pretty grim' there.

one-pause-two   Short for the also used *one-pause-two course*. An officer's initial training course, held at an O.C.T.U. (colloquially: an *octu*). From the 'one-pause-two!' yelled by the instructors dealing with right and left turns.

Op   Operator; e.g., 'He's an op.' (Colloquial.)

oppo   A companion (from '*oppo*site number'); hence, a friend, or even one's wife.

Ops   Operations; Operations Room; Operations Officer. (Colloquial.)

orderly . . .   The R.A.F. has adopted from the Army, which has used them throughout the present century, the following:—

   orderly buff, Orderly Corporal. Not very common.

   orderly dog, Orderly Sergeant. Very common.

   orderly pig, Orderly Officer. Uncommon except among officers.

organize   To 'wangle' something; to 'win' it—i.e., obtain it illicitly. Cf:—

organized   especially *be* or *get organized*, to so arrange a plan or work things as to achieve one's purpose. (Cf. work a swindle.)

Orkneyitis or **scapathy**   That feeling of depression which, after a while, comes to affect many of the airmen stationed in the Orkneys. *Scapathy* is a blend of *Scapa* (Flow) and *apathy*.

out of the blue   An intensive of **in the blue.**

outside view   A view of the target seen from the air.

over the top   Flying either above the **muck** or above the clouds. (It is, therefore, to be sharply differentiated from the Army's use of the same phrase.)

over the wall   Confined to camp; in the guard room. Perhaps because, if one is confined to camp, one may go over the wall (or the fence) if one wishes to get out. Hence, *sixpence* or *sevenpence* or *ninepence* (etc.) *over the wall*, in reference to the number of days' confinement.

owner, the The captain of an aircraft. From the R.N.A.S.

owner's scribe, the That clerk who attends to the Commanding Officer's correspondence. Hence, the Personal Assistant to an Air Marshal or an Air Chief Marshal. (Cf. **owner**.)

P

pack up v.i. E.g., of a 'plane: to cease to function.

packet, buy a (See **bought it . . .**)

pair of white gloves, a A catch-phrase applied to the safe return of all our bombers from a raid. From that delightful old legal custom whereby, to a judge whose calendar is free from crime, his colleagues present a pair of white gloves.

panic, n. and v. (To give way to) a state of excitement or 'jitters.' (Colloquial.)

Paraffin Pete An officer, or an N.C.O., engaged in Airfield Control. One of his duties is to ensure that the flare-path is adequately and timely illuminated.

party A fight in the air; less generally, a bombing raid.

(2) Hence, among the ground-staff: an unusually busy day. (See *Introduction*, para. 11, at end.)

party in the attic A variant of **party**, sense (1), the first nuance. *Attic* because the fight takes place aloft.

passion-killers Airwomen's Service knickers, whether *twilights* or *black-outs*. A wise directive has purposely made them as unromantic in colour and in design as a wise directive could imagine.

pathfinder An airman singularly lucky—or perhaps judicious—in finding women. From the official sense of *pathfinder*: a pilot detailed to go in advance and discover the best direction from which to approach the target.

pea-shooter A machine or a cannon that forms part of the armament of an Allied 'plane.

peck, v.i.   To make a very brief attack and then very abruptly break off the engagement. From the application of kisses that are mere pecks.

peek-a-boo   A shy or timid salute. To *peek* (peep) out and say *boo.*

peelo   A pilot. From the French pronunciation of *pilot.*

Peeping Tom   Any such pilot as can fly skilfully in dirty weather and therefore can, flying from cloud to cloud, espy enemy 'planes while he is crossing his lucid intervals.

Peggy   A Pegasus aero-engine.

penguin   A member of the ground staff, who, like penguins, do not fly; cf. **kiwi.** In 1914–18 the R.F.C. applied the term to 'the wrafs'—the Women's Royal Air Force.

Perce   A Percival ('plane). It is a communication aircraft.

perim   'The perimeter track, tarmac-covered, that runs around the edge of an airfield' (Ward-Jackson).

permanent spats   See **spats.**

Perry   A Peregrine engine. Ground crews.

petal   is the R.A.F.'s synonym of *pansy,* 'effeminate man.'

phoney gen   Information of dubious reliability. See **gen** and *Introduction,* para. 12.

piece of cake, a;   occasionally, *a piece of duff.* An aerial combat in which one obtains an easy victory; a bombing raid with but little 'flak' to overcome. Any task easy to perform. Very often in the form *it's a piece of cake,* which has become a R.A.F. catch-phrase. Cf. the semantics of **cookie** and **party.**

piece of homework   See **homework.**

piece of nice   A very nice—an attractive—girl.

pigs are up, the   The barrage-balloons are in position.

pile in; pile up   To crash in one's 'plane. Also transitively: *pile up one's kite.* To make a *pile* or heap of it.

44

pip-in To synchronize the time in an actually flying aircraft with the time at the 'plane's base (so that the navigational position may be radio-determined). Cf.:—

pip-squeak A 'plane's radiotelephony set. (Pilots' and aircrews'.) At short intervals it emits the noise *pip-squeak*.

Pip, Squeak and Wilfred See Freeman, Hardy, and Willis.

plaster To bomb (a place) heavily. A survival of 1914–18 R.F.C.-R.A.F. slang.

play a flanker To get, unfairly or unjustly, the better of a person. 'If he plays me a flanker over my leave, I'll go to the C.O. about it!' *Flanker* = an outflanking movement; hence, a trick.

playground Parade-ground. Ironic.

play pussy To speed from one cloud to another in order to escape detection or to pounce upon a shadowed enemy aircraft. Therefore cf. **Peeping Tom.**

play the piano To release bombs, one at a time, from an aircraft. Contrast **pull the plug.**

pleep An enemy pilot who refuses aerial combat.

plonk See **A.C. Plonk.**

plumber An armourer.

(2) *The Plumber:* the Engineering Officer. (Officers'.)

Pongo An Army officer. Derogatory: from the name often given to dogs.

poor view See **take a poor view.**

Pop-Eye An observer on duty in a bomber or 'recce' 'plane. His eyes 'pop' because of the strain of constant watching.

P/O Prune See **prune.**

popsie A girl friend. From *Popsie*, diminutive of *Poppy.*

prang A crash landing.

(2) A bombing raid.

45

prang, v. (See *Introduction*, para. 11.) To bomb heavily; intransitively, to crack.

(2) Hence, to knock into, to strike. 'He pranged the iron bedstead.'

(3) Also, to knock: 'He pranged his leg against the bedstead.'

praying mantis Any tail-landing in which the undercarriage fails to descend.

professor, the The Education Officer. (Mostly officers'.)

prog Proctor ('plane). Adopted from Oxford University slang.

prop A propeller. (Adopted from marine-engineers' slang.) It is worth noting that the synonymous *airscrew* has, owing to confusions with *aircrew*, been jettisoned—though too many airmen and officers still persist in using it.

props, get or have one's To become, or to be, a Leading Aircraftman (a rank corresponding to the Army's Lance-Corporal). He wears on the sleeve of his right arm the emblem of a 'plane-propeller.

prune; P/O Prune; prunery A pilot given to unnecessary risks; a Pilot Officer who does this, especially one who has had several 'prangs' (crash-landings); the relevant habit or practice, or an example of *prune's* behaviour.

puff A ladies' man. Perhaps because of his self-advertisement.

pukka gen Genuine or trustworthy information. (See **gen** and *Introduction*, para. 12.)

pull the chocks away! A hangar variant of *get cracking*! Before an aircraft can, prior to taking off, taxi along, the wheel-chocks have to be removed.

pull your finger out! Hurry up! Make a start! (Don't stand gaping with your finger in your mouth!) Among officers there is a variant: *Dedigitate*!

pulpit A cabin; a cockpit. Cf. **conservatory, greenhouse, office.**

pulveriser A Stirling bomber. It can carry very heavy bombs.

pup A pupil pilot; hence, *the Pup's Bible*, The Flying Training Manual.

pusher A 'plane with its engine placed in the rear. Obsolescent type.

put down (of an aircraft or its pilot) To land. Richard Hillary, *The Last Enemy*, 1942.

put the hooks on To charge (a person) with a crime. Hence, *on the hooks*, 'crimed.' From fishing.

put up a black See black, put up a.

pyrotechnic A severe reprimand. Suggested by *rocket*.

Q

queen A 'Waaf,' especially if either pretty or otherwise attractive.

Queen Bee, The The W.A.A.F. officer in charge of a 'Waaf' detachment or unit or camp.

(2) A 'plane that, used for anti-aircraft firing practice, has no crew and is radio-controlled from the ground.

Queen Mary A very long, low-slung, articulated vehicle—a synonym is *artic*—that looks like a huge motor-driven caterpillar but has, in R.A.F. fact, been admirably designed for the transportation of airframes. Besides resembling a caterpillar, it looks, from a distance, like a barge moving on land.

quick squirt A rapid burst of machine-gun fire at or into an enemy 'plane. By itself *squirt* denotes a few such bullets. A frequent statement is, 'I gave him a squirt in the belly,' i.e. from underneath.

quickie or quicky Short for the proceding.

quis (pronounced *kwyce*; often written *kweis* or *kweiss*). Good!; capital!; O.K.! From the Arabic.

R

Raff, the The R.A.F. (Colloquial.) A certain well-known artist member of the R.A.F. uses the drawing-name *Raff*. Cf. **Riff-Raff.**

rat-trap or **mouse-trap** A submarine. (Adopted from the Navy.) To employ an apposite cliché, men in a doomed submarine are 'caught like a rat in a trap.'

rations king, the See **king.**

recce Reconnaissance; hence, a reconnaissance 'plane. (The Army speaks of 'recce battalions'.) The official abbreviation of 'reconnaissance' is *recce*. The R.A.F. also uses the slang variant: *recco*.

rev A revolution (or turn of a wheel).

rev up To make (an engine) go faster. Literally, to get more 'revs' out of it.

Riff-Raff R.A.F. A jocular—sometimes a contemptuous—elaboration of *Raff*.

rigger mortis A useless airman, a stupid 'type.' Punning both *rigger*, an airframe technician, and *rigor mortis*, the implication being that the airman is '*dead, above the ears.*'

rigid See **bind**, v. A deliberate variation of *stiff* in 'to bore a person stiff.'

rigid bind An insufferable bore. (Applied mostly to persons.) See **rigid** and **bind, n.**

Ringer, One—Ringer, Two—Ringer, Three; Half-Ringer—Two-and-a-Half Ringer. Flying Officer — Flight Lieutenant (also *Flight Louie*) — Wing Commander; Pilot Officer — Squadron Leader. From *rings*.

ringmaster A Squadron Leader who actually leads a squadron in the air. From the circus, where the ringmaster superintends the performing animals and other 'turns.'

rings Symbolic of an R.A.F. officer's rank—or, for that matter, of a Naval officer's. (Air Force and Naval officers have rings on their lower sleeve.) (Colloquial.)

48

rock To perturb or startle a person with news or argument. A development from **shake**.

rocket A severe reprimand. Borrowed from Army officers. The R.A.F., however, speaks of *getting the* (not *a*) *rocket*. It blows the recipient sky-high; but cf.:—

Roman-candle landing A bad landing. 'The Control Officer indicates his displeasure by firing off a warning rocket' (Ward-Jackson).

rookette A female recruit. (Not very general.)

rookie or rooky A recruit. Adopted from the Army, this word is obviously a perversion of *recruit*. Cf. **sprog**.

rooty medal Long Service Medal. Adopted from the Regular Army, where it has, since the 1880's, been used in the same sense. *Rooty* is the Regular Army's slang word for bread, and *rooty medal* implies that the wearer has eaten a tremendous aggregate of Service loaves.

ropey Slack; careless of one's appearance; given to blundering.

(2) Inferior (aircraft, meat, etc.); clumsy (e.g., landing); dull (e.g., party). Perhaps from the rope-like smell of inferior tobacco; perhaps from certain obsolete types of aircraft that carried an excess—or what seemed an excess—of ropes.)

S

sack of taters A loadful of bombs, delivered grocery-wise: all at the one time, or at least in very rapid succession.

sardine tin A torpedo-carrying 'plane.

Sasso The S.A.S.O., or Senior Air Staff Officer.

sawn-off Short in stature; especially applied to any Pilot Officer suffering from what is humorously known as 'Duck's disease.'

scapathy See *Orkneyitis*.

scarlet slugs Bofors (anti-aircraft gun) tracer fire.

scat To take off in a hurry, in order to drive off or to disperse enemy 'planes. (See *Introduction*, para. 11.)

schooly Education Officer. (See *Introduction*, para. 6.)

Scotch Mist A phrase that casts a slur upon the addressee's eyesight; it implies that he is suffering from optical illusions. 'Can't you see my tapes? What do you think they are—Scotch mist?' Sometimes *fog* is used instead of *Scotch mist*.

scramble A 'dog-fight,' or mellay in the air.

scramble, to often shortened to *scram*. (The former is official, the latter is slang.) Of pilot and 'plane: to take off.

scrambled egg A Group Captain or higher. From:—

scrambled eggs The gold braid and oak leaves on the dress-service cap of a Group Captain or higher-ranking officer.

scraper ring The half-ring—the middle ring—on a Squadron Leader's tunic-cuffs. 'The origin is technical: in a piston there is a compression ring, an oil-retaining ring and a middle, or scraper, ring' (Ward-Jackson).

screamer A bomb that makes a whistling sound as it comes down. (Colloquial.)

screaming downhill generally as vbl. n. rather than as present participle. Making a power dive, not necessarily—although generally—in a fighter 'plane.

scrounge In the R.A.F. it is used in the sense in which the Army has, since 1914, used *wangle*: to obtain illicitly or by wheedling or by audacious opportunism. Originally a dialect word for 'to filch' (e.g. apples from an orchard).

scrounger One who practises the not wholly ignoble art set forth in the preceding entry.

scrounging The habit or the practice explicit is **scrounge**.

scrub To cancel. 'He'll try to get the posting scrubbed.' To *wipe out*.

scrub around (or *round*). To take evasive action. From the circular motion of scrubbing.

scrubbers! 'Finee!' or 'napoo!,' i.e. over and done with; no longer existing. Perhaps *scrub'er!*, wash it out. From **scrub**.

Second Dickey The Reserve Pilot on a 'plane. Perhaps from *dickey seat*. (It is, however, an unforgivable *faux pas* to call the First Pilot the *First Dickey*: the term does not exist.)

senior scribe The N.C.O. i/c O/R—i.e., the N.C.O. in charge of the orderly room.

sex-appeal bombing The bombing of museums, schools, hospitals —indeed, of civilians in general.

Shagbat A Walrus 'plane. A bat flies; *walrus* whiskers are shaggy.

shake To startle; to perturb; to set thinking anxiously; to stir (a person) out of his complacency. Proleptic. Especially in the virtual catch-phrase, 'That shook him.'

shaky do Any activity or incident to which grave exception is or should be taken; a bungled affair.

shed is colloquial for: hangar.

ship A 'plane—not only a flying ship but any aircraft.

ships that pass in the night Officers and airmen serving only 'for the duration.' Regulars'.

shit Very dirty weather.

shoot a—or the—line To boast; to exaggerate; to talk excessively on a subject. (See *Introduction*, para. 13.) Both 'shooting a line' and 'line-shooter' occur in Richard Hillary's fine book, *The Last Enemy*, 1942.

shoot down; shoot down in flames; shoot down from a great height To defeat in an argument; to be right on a question of procedure, dress, drill, etc. (See *Introduction*, para. 13.) The first—though far from colourless—is the weakest; the second connotes a victory that utterly routs the opponent—as does the third, with the added connotation of calm and/or great intellectual superiority in the victor. Cf.:—

shoot up To dive upon or fly very low over a building as though one were about to attack it. (Colloquial.) Pupil pilots do this as part of their training; any unthinking pilot is likely to do it to his home, his fiancée's home, his parents' home, his home town.

shooting gallery See **lines book**.

shot down in flames As in shoot down.
        (2) Hence; jilted; crossed in love.

shot up Very drunk; whereas a person *shot to ribbons* is so drunk as to be helpless and hopeless. From aerial warfare.

showery, it's; what a shower! Catch-phrase addressed to one who has just been making a bad mistake. Proleptic of the cold douche he will probably receive from an irate superior.

Sid Walker gang A crash salvage party. One of Cockney comedian Sid Walker's most famous songs is, 'Day after day, I'm on my way, Any rags, bottles, or bones?'

silver sausage A barrage balloon.

skipper The captain of an aircraft. (Colloquial.)

skirt patrol A search for a female companion—any suitable female. Mostly pilots' and aircrews'.

skypiece Smoke-trails. Punning on *landscape*.

sky-pilot A padre. Common to all three Services; ex-civilian slang.

sling one up See **fling one up**.

sling round To test a 'plane in the air. From the test pilot's tricks.

smashing job A very fine aircraft; a task excellently performed; a girl exceedingly easy on the eye. *Job* is R.A.F. for 'thing, matter, affair'; *smashing* has been adopted from the Army, which took it from Cockney slang.

smile-please run A photo-reconnaissance flight. From professional photographers' 'Smile, please!'

smoothie (or -*y*) One who thinks himself a successful ladies' man. Cf. Australian *smoodger*, a wheedler or cajoler.

snake A lively or noisy party. Hence, *out on the snake*, at a party. Cf. **snake-charmers**.

snake; snake about 'To take evasive action when pursued by enemy fighters or when illuminated by searchlights and engaged by ack-ack' (Hunt and Pringle). (Colloquial.)

snake-charmers A dance band. A snake-charmer employs music. Cf. **snake**, n.

snargasher A training aircraft. Canadian pilots'. A corruption of *tarmac-smasher*; clumsy landings are frequent among pupil pilots.

snogging, go or be To go—to be—courting a girl; to go—or be—love-making. *Snog* is perhaps a blend of *snug* and *cod* (to flatter or 'kid' a person).

snoop To be a Service Policeman; more generally, to be actively prosecuting one's S.P. duties. From general slang, where it = to be pryingly inquisitive.

snooper or **snoop** A member of the Service Police. See also **Gestapo**.

soggy type A 'wet'—a dull or stupid or silly person. From soggy ground.

soup Dirty weather. Cf. **shit**.

spam medal See **Naffy gong**.

Sparks; sparks Wireless operator: the former in address; the latter, otherwise. Adopted from the Navy of 1914–18, it has long been general slang. From the electric sparks emitted from certain instruments.

spawny Very lucky. 'He was spawny to get that compassionate leave so easily.' *Spawny* = fertile in spawn; fertility = richness = good fortune.

Spit A Spitfire fighter 'plane. Obviously an abbreviation; also, however, with a reference to the fact that this 'plane *spits* fire (or bullets). Hence, the synonymous *Spitter*.

spit-and-polish parade   A parade inspection by a C.O. or an A.C.O.

split-arse   This adjective denotes 'daring' or 'addicted to stunting,' hence 'reckless—dashingly reckless.' Deriving from *full-split* (at full speed), it occurs in numerous combinations, e.g.:—

split-arse cap. The field-service, as opposed to the peaked dress-service, cap.

split-arse landing. A daring or very chancy landing.

split-arse merchant; split-arse pilot; a test pilot; a stunt pilot.

split-arse turn. A particularly hazardous manœuvre, or at least a manœuvre that would be very risky except to an 'ace.'

Split-arse dates from the old R.F.C. days. Semantically, it is not unconnected with 'the splits.'

spout   Barrel of a rifle or a gun. *One up the spout*, a bullet in the breech.

sprog   A recruit. (See *Introduction*, para. 7, end.)

(2) Hence, an adjective: new; newly promoted: as in 'a sprog uniform,' 'a sprog corporal.'

spud-basher   An airman engaged in potato-peeling when, especially if he's doing 'jankers,' he is on a cookhouse fatigue. See **basher**.

spun in   This phrase is applied to one who has—especially if he admits that he has—committed a technical error. (To allow one's 'plane to spin is to court disaster.)

(2) Also literally: to have failed to get out of a spin; to crash.

squadron bleeder   A Squadron Leader. By an entirely good-natured rhyming pun.

Squadron Leader Swill   The Administrative Officer (S/L admin.) on a Station. One of his multitudinous duties is the disposal of swill.

square-bashing and **swede-bashing;** synonymous with the latter is *turnip-bashing*. Drill on the square or parade-ground; field training, which often takes recruits into the fields and hedgerows.

squeeze the teat See **teat**.

squirt See **quick squirt**.

(2) A jet-propelled 'plane. First heard by the compiler on May 31, 1944. Punning *jet*.

squo A *Squa*dron *O*fficer (a W.A.A.F. officer that = a R.A.F. Squadron Leader).

stand-in The benevolent person mentioned in:—

stand in for (a person). To take his place, do his duty for him. (Colloquial.) From standing in the ranks in his stead.

Stationmaster Station Commander. From the railway title.

Stationmaster's meetings Conferences convened and presided-over by the Station Commander.

steam, v.i. To work hard and effectually. When water steams freely, it is boiling.

stick = joy-stick Aircraft control-lever. The longer form dates from the R.F.C. era: from the thrill one gets in handling it.

(2) A load of bombs dropped all at the one time: the bombs land in a straight line. (Colloquial.)

stiffener One who binds you rigid. Cf. 'to bore a person stiff.'

stooge, v. often as vbl. n., *stooging*. To be on patrol. From:—

stooge, n. A deputy; an assistant (e.g., pilot); a *stand-in*. Adopted from the Army, it derives from *student* or, more probably, *studious*.

stooge about (or **around**) A variant of **stooge,** v.

(2) To delay one's landing.

store-basher   An Equipment Assistant. See **basher** and cf. **clock basher, tin basher.**

Store Basher's Bible, the   Air Publication No. 830; vol. I is entitled *Equipment Regulations*, vol. II: *Storage and Packing*, vol. III: *Scales of R.A.F. Equipment.*

strafe, n. and v.   (To) attack. Except in *ground-strafe*, the word is now little used. (For history and origin, see Brophy and Partridge, *Songs and Slang of the British Soldier*: 1914–1918.)

stringbag   A Swordfish—or an Albacore—'plane, used by the F.A.A. From 'Stringbag the Sailor.' (Hunt and Pringle.)

stuff   Mostly in 'There's (or, there was) a lot of stuff going across': many 'planes . . ., and in 'Heavy stuff' (heavy bombers).

Sun   The Sunderland flying-boat. From the official abbreviation.

supercharged   In a drunken state.

swede   A green recruit; hence, any airman with a countrified manner or in the habit of speaking dialect. Cf.:—

swede- (or **turnip-**) **bashing**   See **square-bashing.**

swindle   A 'wangle'; a cunning piece of work.

synthetic   Artificial; not genuine. Applied to, e.g., ground as opposed to air training. Cf. the *ersatz* (substitute; hence, inferior) of 1914–18.

T

Tail-End Charlie   Nickname of the rear gunner.

(2) By extension; the rear 'plane in a formation.

take a dim view   An intensive form of:—

take a poor view (of)   To condemn. (Colloquial.) (Adopted from the Army.)

take it on   Of a 'plane: to climb rapidly.

take the can back is an occasional variant of **carry the can.**

tangled in the soup, to be To be lost, or to go astray, in a fog. (See *Introduction*, para. 11.)

tapes, get or **have one's** To become, or to be, a corporal. Hence *get one's third* (tape), to become a sergeant.

tap in, v.i. To enjoy oneself. ' "Cobber" Kain had only to shout into his radio, "Enemy aircraft ahead: let's tap in," and the call would be answered with a rousing "Tally-ho!" . . . ("Tap in" was R.A.F. slang in France for "have a good time")', Noel Monks, *Squadrons Up*, 1940.

taps The 'gadgets'—controls, indicators, etc.—in the cabin or the cockpit of a 'plane.

target for to-night, one's One's girl friend.

tatered Depressed or exasperated by unexciting patrols. (Pilots' and aircrews'.) A potato, though—like the patrol—exceedingly useful, can become monotonous.

taters See sack . . .

taxi A 'plane that will carry a small number of passengers.

taxi-driver An instructor at a school of training in navigation.

taxidermist, go and see a A R.A.F. variation, introduced in 1943, of the general low catch-phrase, *go and get stuffed*. For 'to *stuff*,' see *stuff*, v., in my *A Dictionary of Slang*. A taxidermist stuffs the skins of eviscerated animals and birds. There is a story to the effect that a certain airman, soon after he reached his first station, was asked his trade, and when he answered 'Taxidermist,' the S.W.O. looked hard at him; very shortly afterwards the airman was posted overseas.

tear (a person) off a strip To reprimand, or to scold, severely. 'The "Stationmaster" tore him off a strip for dressing in so slovenly a way.' Off his self-satisfaction.

teased out Exhausted, or at least very tired; after a long duty on patrol or raid. From teasing out of a rope: cf. '*frayed* nerves.'

teat Especially in *squeeze the teat*, to press that electric button in an aircraft which fires the machine-guns. The phrase occurs in Noel Monk's *Squadrons Up*, 1940.

tee up! Get ready! Cf. the Army's *to have* (a thing) *teed up* or ready. From golf.

That shook him See shake.

that thing is (or **was**) **wild** That 'plane flies (or flew) much faster than I thought (or had thought) it did. Probably an allusion to horses.

three months' bumps A three months' course of training in flying. Cf. **circuits and bumps**.

three-pointer An excellent landing. (Colloquial; i.e., on all three points (the wheels).)

throw one up See fling one up.

ticket A pilot's certificate. From the Merchant Service and Navy via the R.N.A.S.

tiggerty-boo Correct; in order. *Tiggerty* from Hindustani *teega*; for the second element, cf. **peek-a-boo**.

tin basher A metal worker in the R.A.F. See basher.

tin fish A torpedo. From the Navy and antedating 1914. Cf. **mouldy**.

tit A gun-button. (*Teat* in its common mispronunciation.)
(2) Hence, any finger-pressed button—e.g., that of an electric bell.

titfa or **titfer** A cap; a steel hat. Merely a specialization of the civilian *titfer*, which shortens rhyming-slang *tit-for-tat* (hat).

toffee-nose (or **-nosed**) Supercilious; stand-offish; superior. 'So you've gone all toffee-nose and won't come with us!' From *toff*, 'a gentleman,' and a pridefully high-held nose.

tool along To fly aimlessly; hence, to walk aimlessly. From coaching or other horse-driving.

tools A slangy synonym of **irons**.

topside (Flying) in the air; airborne.

totem-pole A thus shaped piece of airfield-lighting equipment. Mainly officers'.

touch-bottom A crash landing. The 'plane can get no lower down. From:—

touch bottom, v. To make a crash-landing. By meiosis.

touch down To land. From football. (Contrast preceding entry.)

toy A trainer aircraft; a Link Trainer. Cf.:—

toys 'The mechanical parts of a 'plane so beloved by the armourers and flight mechanics who care for the machines.' (Hunt and Pringle, *Service Slang*, 1943.)

train-driver The officer in charge of a large formation of 'planes.

Trenchard brat A Royal Air Force boy apprentice. Since 1920, when Lord Trenchard introduced the apprenticeship system; obsolescent since September, 1939.

tricycle A 'plane with a three-wheeled undercarriage. Now colloquial.

trousers The streamline covering of the undercarriage legs of certain types of 'plane; the 'planes themselves are said to be *trousered*. Cf. **spats**.

tug A 'plane to which gliders are attached.

turn up the wick To open the throttle (also *go through the gate*). It's an easy transition from getting a better light to getting a higher speed.

turnip-bashing See the **square-bashing** entry.

twilights A Waaf's pair of summer-weight knickers, lighter coloured than **black-outs**.

Two-and-a-Half Ringer See **Ringer**.

Type A person, whether in the R.A.F. itself or in the Army or the Navy. E.g., 'He's a good type'—'That fellow's a poor (or *ropey*) type.' Perhaps from Free French officers' use of the general French slang *type*, a chap, a fellow; but probably from 'type of aircraft.'

U

umbrella A parachute.

umbrella man A parachutist.

up the creek Off one's course; lost on patrol—hence, on a merry night-out. From the Navy: up a creek instead of in a proper or regular anchorage.

up top Flying high.

upstairs (Flying) in the air; airborne. Synonymous with **topside**.

U.S. (Of a person) unavailable or inadequate. From the official abbreviation, u/s (or U/S), 'unserviceable.'

use your loaf! Use your brains! *Loaf* is short for *loaf of bread*, rhyming slang for 'head.' (Adopted from the Army.)

V

Vic 'The Vickers-Victoria or Valencia Troop Carrier and Transport Aircraft' (Ward-Jackson).

visiting-card A bomb. Mostly in *Leave one's visiting card* (or *cards*). As the civilian drops visiting cards into tray or salver, so the airman drops bombs on enemy or enemy-occupied territory.

W

Waaf pronounced and often written *Waff*. A member of the Women's Auxiliary Air Force. Hence the *Waafery* (or *Waffery*): W.A.A.F. billets; W.A.A.F. office in a Station Headquarters building.

waafize, vi. and vt.   To substitute 'Waafs' for airmen (in a unit—a station, etc.). 'Are you going to waafize?' 'We've been waafized.'

wad   See **char.**

waffle; waffling   (To be) out of control; applied to a 'plane that is spinning or losing height.

(2) In many squadrons, however, *waffle* is 'to cruise along unconcernedly and indecisively.'

wallah   A chap or fellow. Borrowed from the Army. From Hindustani (cf. the Arabic *walad*). See *A Dictionary of Slang and Unconventional English.*

wallop   Beer. Common to all three Services, the word has been adopted from public-house slang. It gives one a *kick.*

wanks   Strong liquor. Origin?

want   See **do you want . . .**

warrant, have got one's   To have been promoted Warrant Officer. (Colloquial.)

watch basher   See **clock basher.**

wear it   To tolerate; to permit. 'The S.W.O. wouldn't wear it when I asked for extra leave.' Adopted from Midland slang: the wearing of factory-made garments.

weaving, get   To busy oneself. It corresponds with the Army's *get cracking,* which is common in the R.A.F. too. From the 'weaving' or dodging of a 'plane to avoid the fire of the enemy.

Week-End Air Force, the   Used from 1925 (the year of its inception) until the outbreak of war for the Auxiliary Air Force, formed of citizens who selflessly gave their week-ends and other spare time in order to reinforce the R.A.F.

What do you think that is—fog (or Scotch mist)?   See **Scotch mist.**

What's cooking?   What is happening? Adopted from U.S.A. From 'What is that smell—what's *cooking*?': asked so very often by so many husbands.

61

wheels down! Get ready—especially, ready to leave a bus, tram, train. From lowering the wheels, preparatory to landing.

Whirligig Whirlwind fighter 'plane. By affectionate depreciation.

whistle, v.i. To depart hurriedly. Applied, e.g., to a fighter squadron hurriedly taking off in order to attack enemy bombers. From the whistling sound produced by particularly rapid movement.

whistled In a state of intoxication—usually, of mild intoxication, wherein one tends to whistle cheerfully and perhaps discordantly.

whistler A high-explosive bomb as it comes down. (Colloquial.)

whizzbang A fighter 'plane pursuing an enemy bomber 'plane. Reminiscent of that very rapid German field-gun, the '77,' which (or rather, its shell) our men in 1914–18 called by this name.

wife Fiancée; 'girl'; mistress.

Wimpey A Wellington bomber 'plane. In a well-known series of comic cartoons, Mr. J. *Wellington Wimpey* is the esteemed partner of Popeye the Sailor.

windmill Synonymous with **egg-whisk.**

Wingco *Wing Com*mander. Also *Winco.*

wizard Excellent, superlative; beautiful; very ingenious. Adopted from civilian slang.

wom A *W/O/M,* i.e. a Wireless Operator (Mechanic). Cf. **wop** and **wopag.**

woof To open the throttle very quickly. From:—
(2) To gobble one's food; itself from 'to *wolf* one's food.'

wop A wireless operator. From the official abbreviation, *W/Op.*

wopag A wireless operator and air gunner. From the official abbreviation *W.Op/A.G.*

work a swindle To effect a 'wangle'; to obtain something illicitly. Cf. **organize**.

Works and Bricks is colloquial for the Air Ministry Works Directorate, which controls the maintenance as well as the construction of aerodromes, hangars, offices, etc.

wrap up To crash (a 'plane).

wrapped up Synonymous with **buttoned up**, it = under perfect control; most satisfactorily arranged. 'He has the job buttoned up *or* wrapped up.'

write-off A crashed 'plane; equipment beyond repair. It must be *written off* as no longer serviceable and therefore to be no longer kept on the inventory.

write oneself off To get killed. Cf. **write-off** and:—

written off (Of a 'plane) crashed beyond repair; hence (of a person), killed. Cf. **write-off**.

Y

yellow doughnut 'The small collapsible dinghy carried on modern aircraft—it looks like a doughnut from the air' (Hunt and Pringle, *Service Slang*, 1943).

yellow peril A trainer aircraft. (Not a Link Trainer, but a proper 'plane.) From its colour and from that 'yellow streak' in its character which it may display when it is unskilfully handled.

yob A raw recruit (cf. **sprog**); a very much countrified airman (cf. **swede**). This word has mystified many etymologists: it's simply backslang for *boy*. In civilian slang, where it has existed throughout the twentieth century (and probably longer), it connotes loutishness.

you know what you can do —occasionally, **what to do**—**with it!** The semantics are implicit in a full 'definition': *I* don't care what you do about it (or, with it)—and indeed, so far as I'm concerned, you can insert it in your anus. This catch-phrase has been adopted from civil life, where it became general about 1930.

You're holding up production You're getting in the way; you're wasting time; you're not being very helpful.

You've been 'You've had it' as applied to a trip in an aircraft, or to an interesting visit, that has been cancelled.

You've had it! See **had it.**